R-4195-OSD/A/AF

Civil-Military Relations and National Security Thinking in Czechoslovakia

A Conference Report

Thomas S. Szayna, James B. Steinberg

Prepared for the
Office of the Secretary of Defense
United States Army
United States Air Force

RAND

PREFACE

This Report analyzes the discussions between Czechoslovak and U.S. government officials and security experts during a workshop on "Civil-Military Relations and the Development of National Security Policy in the United States and the Czech and Slovak Federal Republic (CSFR)," held in Prague, CSFR, on May 5–7, 1991. The workshop was one of a series of meetings sponsored by RAND in Eastern Europe that was designed to establish a broad dialogue between American policymakers and the new officials in charge of security matters in the region. The Czechoslovak cosponsor of this workshop was the Institute of International Relations.

This Report should interest U.S. policymakers and analysts concerned with the Czechoslovak military and the evolution of East European foreign and security policies. This work was conducted as part of the concept-formulation and research-support activities of RAND's three federally funded research and development centers: Project AIR FORCE, sponsored by the United States Air Force; the Arroyo Center, sponsored by the United States Army; and the National Defense Research Institute (NDRI), sponsored by the Office of the Secretary of Defense and the Joint Staff. The work was overseen by RAND's International Policy Department.

SUMMARY

This Report summarizes the results of a workshop entitled "Civil-Military Relations and the Development of National Security Policy in the United States and the Czech and Slovak Federal Republic (CSFR)," held in Prague, CSFR, on May 5–7, 1991, and sponsored by RAND and the CSFR Institute of International Relations. The workshop was devoted to the issues of civil-military relations and national security policy in the new, post-Communist Czechoslovakia.

Throughout Eastern Europe, civil-military relations are undergoing fundamental changes as the new civilian officials assert control over military establishments previously controlled by ruling Communist parties. The relative inexperience of,the new officials makes the process more difficult. In the Czechoslovak case, the deep antimilitary outlooks prevalent in the society, the ethnic conflict that has the potential to break the state apart, the ambivalence of some of the current top officials toward the military as a component of security policy, and the brevity of the transition from a Communist to a democratic system further complicate the process.

Despite these problems, the workshop demonstrated the considerable evolution of Czechoslovak security policy institutions. The Czechoslovak military is evolving into a genuine state institution. The Federal Assembly (Czechoslovak parliament) has achieved substantial, if still incomplete, control over the military through legislative action, budgetary pressure, and the formation of a General Inspectorate of the Armed Forces subordinate only to the Federal Assembly. Old mechanisms of Communist control over the armed forces, such as the Main Political Administration and military counterintelligence, have been abolished or fundamentally restructured, while sweeping personnel changes, accompanied by screenings of all officers, have altered the upper ranks of the military. The Ministry of Defense has also instituted another important reform, separating the functions between the political-administrative activities performed increasingly by civilians and the command of the troops carried out by the General Staff. An increasing number of civilians occupy influential posts within the Ministry of Defense, including the Defense Minister and a Deputy Defense Minister.

Workshop discussions largely avoided the issue of ethnic conflict, which was clearly an uncomfortable topic for the Czechoslovak side. However, the matter was always in the background. Czechoslovak participants downplayed the role of Slovak splinter groups within the armed forces, and they avoided altogether the issue of Slovak territorial militia. Although the conference did not address the issue directly, the spread of ethnic conflict to the military is bound to have a divisive influence on the armed forces as well as damage the functioning, efficiency, and cohesion of the Czechoslovak military.

With regard to national security policy, workshop discussions illustrated the Czechoslovak commitment to integrating the country into Western political, economic, and security structures. These ideas are a consequence of the general goal underlying the Czechoslovak transformation: to establish a liberal democracy and a free market economy. Although Czechoslovak foreign policy has evolved and matured greatly since the political changes in November 1989, its main thrust of creating a new, all-European collective security system based on institutionalizing the Conference on Security and Cooperation in Europe (CSCE) process had remained at the time of the conference. Reasons for this approach stem from historical failure of the alliances to guarantee Czechoslovak security and continued uncertainty in Europe, including the problems with integrating Germany, instability in the former USSR, and the specter of militarized ethnic conflict in Eastern Europe. Since the conference took place, the Czechoslovak position has changed to emphasize NATO as the basis for a future security organization for all of Europe—a position similar to that of Poland and Hungary.

For the Czechoslovak participants, a collective security system seemed to be the only available option to guarantee Czechoslovak security in the long run, since, in their view, neutrality only made sense during the Cold War, and at the time of the conference, NATO had been unwilling to extend even associate membership to Czechoslovakia. The last point was a source of thinly disguised disappointment to Czechoslovak participants, though U.S. participants argued that the rebuff did not necessarily represent the last word on the issue. Events since the workshop—the breakup of the former USSR and the creation of the North Atlantic Cooperation Council—have rendered some of the Czechoslovak fears obsolete.

Czechoslovakia adopted a new military doctrine in spring 1991 that reflects the country's pro-Western orientation. The doctrine envisions an all-around territorial defense using only Czechoslovak resources. Although the doctrine is in some ways a throwback to the Czechoslovak doctrinal deliberations in the mid–1960s, its adoption has had the important consequence of having military units begin redeploying to the east. Czechoslovak participants had no illusions about the military potential of their country. Their armed forces are constrained by relatively limited material, operational, and economic potential. These constraints led to Czechoslovak advocacy for further institutionalizing the CSCE, and they are likely to contribute to further Czechoslovak support for a rapid creation of a new European collective security organization.

ACKNOWLEDGMENTS

The authors would like to thank Steven Popper of RAND and A. Ross Johnson of Radio Free Europe/Radio Liberty Research Institute for their constructive comments on an earlier draft of this Report.

CONTENTS

1. INTRODUCTION

The collapse of Communist rule has profoundly altered the political landscape in the countries of Eastern Europe. The reorientation toward democratic, pluralistic political rule and market-oriented economies has been accompanied by a parallel reorientation in foreign and security policies. East European attempts to redefine the institutions dealing with national security must be seen against this background of radical change.

For the first time in over four decades, the East Europeans are able to arrange their political institutions on the basis of popular wishes and to formulate sovereign foreign and defense policies. Yet the new officials in the region came to power having little experience in foreign and defense policy matters. The veil of secrecy that surrounded national security under Communist rule has led to an almost complete lack of prior experience among the new, non-Communist political leaderships. Moreover, many of the new officials harbored a good deal of skepticism toward the military that was rooted in their experience with the military as a tool of domestic repression and the armed wing of the Communist party. Furthermore, they had formed their views on foreign and security affairs while in the opposition in the 1970s and the 1980s. Their intellectual roots were often based in the Helsinki process and the détente experience, with its emphasis on pan-Europeanism and collective security. Similarly, many of the contacts these groups enjoyed with the West were largely through the West European left and the peace movement of the late 1970s and early 1980s.

As a result, many of the new officials in the region have been engaged in a crash course in national security thinking while simultaneously redefining civil-military relations and national security doctrines. They must confront these challenges in a radically new and often uncertain environment. Not only are these countries faced with fundamental economic transformation, social upheaval, and the establishment of new political systems, but they must seek to assess the ramifications of German unification, West European integration, and the disintegration of the former USSR. It is a time of sweeping change that has few parallels.

Against this backdrop, RAND has initiated a series of workshops with the new political leaders in the region. An initial workshop was held in February 1990 in Budapest, Hungary.[1] A second workshop was held in June 1990 in Warsaw, Poland.[2] This Report provides an analytical summary of the third workshop, held in Prague, Czechoslovakia (CSFR),[3] in May 1991. While the specific agenda of each workshop varied somewhat, they all centered on the twin themes of civil-military relations and the integration of these countries into a new European security system.

Although Czechoslovakia has many features in common with other East European countries, the Czechoslovak case has some unique characteristics. First, in contrast to other East European countries, the Czechoslovak state consists of two main ethnic groups, each of which enjoys an ethnoterritorial status as well as several minor ethnic groups (most important of whom are the Hungarians). Ethnic conflict had simmered under the surface during the Communist period, but it reemerged into the open immediately following the ouster of Communists from top political posts, and it has become the dominant issue in contemporary Czechoslovakia, threatening the existence of the state. Second, many in Czechoslovakia hold a deeply ingrained antimilitary outlook that complicates civil-military relations. The long-standing, historically based antimilitary feelings in Czechoslovakia have no parallel in any other country in Eastern Europe. Third, since the 1970s, the open opposition to the Communist rule in Czechoslovakia had been limited mainly to intellectuals, especially cultural figures, who often espoused pacifist ideas. When this group assumed positions of power following the ouster of Communists, a deep gap in perceptions on national security emerged between the military and the new civilian political leaders. Czechoslovakia presents a dramatic case of the impact of the Helsinki legacy on current leaders in Eastern Europe, which manifested itself in Czechoslovakia's role as perhaps the staunchest supporter of institutionalizing the CSCE process. Finally, Czechoslovakia did not go through an extended transition period from a Brezhnevite system to a democratic

---

[1]See Keith W. Crane, Steven W. Popper, and Barbara A. Kliszewski, *Civil-Military Relations in a Multiparty Democracy: Report of a Conference Organized by the RAND Corporation and the Hungarian Institute of International Affairs,* RAND, R-3941-RC, August 1990.

[2]See Ronald D. Asmus and Thomas S. Szayna, *Polish National Security Thinking in a Changing Europe: A Conference Report,* RAND, R-4056-FF, 1991.

[3]The official name of the country was changed in April 1990 to the Czech and Slovak Federal Republic. For reasons of clarity and convenience, the name Czechoslovakia is used in this Report.

one (as happened in Hungary and Poland). The whole transition stage amounted to only a few months. The brevity of the transition has affected policy, both in conception and execution. For example, in the foreign policy realm, there was no gradual widening of the consensus-building process.

The workshop took place a year and a half after the political changes of November–December 1989, and the situation and the atmosphere already differed qualitatively from those of similar earlier workshops held in Hungary and Poland. By the time of the workshop, free presidential and parliamentary elections had removed the Communist party from positions of power. A non-Communist, Foreign Minister Jiri Dienstbier, had been appointed as early as December 1989, and Czechoslovak foreign policy had adopted a pro-Western and then staunchly Atlanticist course. A civilian non-Communist, Lubos Dobrovsky, assumed the post of the Defense Minister in October 1990, replacing a transitional Communist figure, and was followed by a further influx of civilians into top positions of the Defense Ministry. Even before Dobrovsky became Defense Minister, the military's mission had changed from its previous role as a component of the Warsaw Pact to purely defensive operations in order to safeguard national territory.

These were the specific circumstances when the U.S.-Czechoslovak workshop, entitled "Civil-Military Relations and the Development of National Security Policy in the United States and the Czech and Slovak Federal Republic," took place. The workshop was initiated and sponsored on the U.S. side by RAND. The Institute of International Relations, an advisory body on foreign policy to the Czechoslovak government, was the Czechoslovak sponsor. The workshop was held in Prague on May 5–7, 1991, and it consisted of one and a half days of discussions. Participants from the United States included active and retired senior military figures and civilian officials from the United States Department of Defense, researchers from RAND, and specialists dealing with Eastern Europe. Participants from Czechoslovakia included senior military figures, civilian officials from the Ministries of Defense and Foreign Affairs, members of the Federal Assembly, scholars from the Czechoslovak Institute of International Relations, and other Czechoslovak officials and experts in security studies (see Appendix A for the full list of participants).

The majority of Czechoslovak participants were Czechs, though there were also several Slovaks present, as well as one Hungarian. The Czechoslovak civilians came from diverse backgrounds: individuals associated with the "Prague Spring" in 1968 now back in influential posts after a 20-year hiatus; activists from the intellectual-dominated opposition of the late 1970s and 1980s; a few who had managed to continue some involvement in their fields after 1968 despite being active in the "Prague Spring"; as well as one who had recently returned to Czechoslovakia after two decades at a U.S. university. Czechoslovak military representatives came from two distinct backgrounds. Some of them from the former Communist military establishment were now struggling to redefine their role in a post-Communist world. Others had been purged from the military after 1968 and had recently been reactivated.

The workshop took place during a time of consolidating civilian control over the Ministry of Defense, and there were no major, publicly voiced, issue-based disagreements between the military and civilians. If anything, differences surfaced along institutional lines (parliament and the Ministry of Defense), though they were not limited to these sides. Signs of tension between the Czechoslovak military and civilian participants emerged in a latent form, as some civilians showed little sensitivity toward the military. Some U.S. participants felt that the Czechoslovak civilian participants showed less understanding for the need of the military to be accepted in a new role in the society than did the Polish and Hungarian participants at the earlier RAND workshops in Hungary and Poland. In addition, some U.S. participants felt that the Czechoslovak representatives appeared to be not as far along in grappling with security issues under the radically altered circumstances as were the officials in Poland and Hungary at the time of the RAND workshops in those countries. One probable reason for the relative backwardness of the Czechoslovak officials may be the presence of a "counter-elite," namely the military and civilian officials active in the late 1960s who had been purged following the Soviet-led invasion in 1968. These officials have become quite influential since the ouster of the old regime, and their views—characterized by a certain "time warp" and a tendency to try to revive concepts from the 1960s that have questionable relevance today—may actually make it more difficult for Czechoslovakia to adapt to the radically new security environment of the 1990s.

The workshop was divided into three sessions: (1) Establishing Civilian Control of the Military, (2) Defining National Goals and Policies, and (3) CSFR and U.S. Perspectives on Security in Central Europe. A more detailed agenda can be found in Appendix B. The proceedings of the workshop are summarized in an issue-based format that integrates opinions expressed over the course of the two days. Since many U.S. presentations were devoted to explaining how the U.S. system works, they are not summarized in this Report.

Instead, this Report focuses on issues concerning Czechoslovak policies and practices with the aim of sharing these discussions with a wider audience of U.S. and other scholars and policymakers.

The workshop was held on a not-for-attribution basis. The participants are therefore identified only by country of origin and as civilians or military. Individual opinions expressed at the workshop are clearly noted as such in the Report.

The failed coup attempt in the former USSR took place a few months after the workshop, radically changing the international situation and rendering many of the deliberations at the workshop obsolete. For example, the discussions regarding the threat perception from the former USSR and the expectation of a continued strong role by the USSR in Eastern Europe have been overtaken by events. Nevertheless, these discussions are included in this Report as a matter of record and to illustrate the evolution in Czechoslovak thinking on security matters.

2. CIVIL-MILITARY RELATIONS

The evolution of civil-military relations in Czechoslovakia since the collapse of the Communist regime must be seen in the context of several interrelated factors: the overall transformation of the relationship between the military and the society in Czechoslovakia, the complicity of the Czechoslovak military in upholding the Communist regime in the past, and Czechoslovakia's transition to a liberal democracy.[1] Each of these issues was touched on during the workshop. Before these issues are discussed, a short review of the background is in order.

The revolution in Czechoslovakia took place in November and December 1989, after the developments in Poland, Hungary, and East Germany already had undermined Communist control in much of Eastern Europe, and after the Soviet Union had made clear in words and actions that it was not prepared to intervene to save the *ancien regimes*. The timing of Czechoslovakia's political transformation undoubtedly contributed to the rapid pace of change. A month and a half after the initial demonstrations that sparked the change, Vaclav Havel, the most prominent member of the opposition, became President. An interim government was created, and following the June 1990 legislative elections came the first democratically chosen government since 1948. The new government was composed primarily of representatives from the broad-based anti-Communist coalition (Civic Forum in the Czech lands and the Public Against Violence [PAV] in Slovakia).

Initially, Civic Forum and PAV demanded a civilian defense minister, but, in deference to Soviet security concerns, they accepted the appointment of a uniformed officer, then Deputy Defense Minister and Chief of the General Staff, Lieutenant General Miroslav Vacek. Vacek replaced General Milan Vaclavik, who lost all credibility in the immediate aftermath of the demonstrations, when he appeared to support retaining the Communist regime. Vacek implemented a far-reaching program of military reform, and he seems to have won a measure of genuine respect from the new government. Although the new government focused on the Interior Ministry to secure the politi-

---

[1]For a more detailed look at the evolution of civil-military relations in Czechoslovakia since the ouster of the old regime, see Thomas S. Szayna, *The Military in a Postcommunist Czechoslovakia*, RAND, N-3412-USDP, 1992.

6

cal changes during the first half of 1990, the new leaders did not ignore the military and took gradual steps to make it accountable to the government, to depoliticize it, and to transform it into an institution serving the Czechoslovak state, not the discredited Communist party.

Vacek's reforms went quite a long way toward achieving these goals. However, Havel and his advisers never hid their intent to replace Vacek with a civilian, as part of the overall transition toward a liberal democratic system in Czechoslovakia. Following revelations that appeared to implicate Vacek in plans for a military crackdown in November 1989, and amidst increasing legislative criticism of Vacek for the slow pace of military reform, Havel decided that the time to make the change had arrived.

In October 1990, Lubos Dobrovsky, a civilian closely associated with Havel, replaced Vacek. Dobrovsky and his aides increased the civilian staff of the Ministry of Defense and separated it functionally from actual troop command. As part of a new military doctrine, adopted in March 1991, the Czechoslovak military began to redeploy forces away from its previous anti-NATO orientation and toward the concept of "defense of all borders." Although the process of sweeping personnel changes in the upper ranks of the military began in late 1989, Dobrovsky pushed the effort forward in the spring of 1991.

THE PRESTIGE PROBLEM

In Czechoslovakia, the military's prestige is quite low. This view was shared by all the CSFR conference participants, and it poses a serious challenge to developing effective civil-military relations.

The public's low esteem for the military stems from several interrelated factors. First, as a state institution associated with the federal government, the military suffers from the public's general weak attachment to those institutions. A state composed mainly of Czechs and Slovaks dates only from the end of the First World War. It is a fragile creation with little historical basis and, like Yugoslavia, has failed to develop as great an internal cohesion as is common to many other East (or West) European countries. Although there are strong ethnic nationalist sentiments in the Czech lands and in Slovakia, identification with the state is limited, especially in Slovakia.

Second, the military is associated by many with the rule of foreign powers. In the Czech lands, this sentiment dates back to the disappearance of the Bohemian state in the 17th century and the dominance of military forces by Germany and the Austro-Hungarian Empire. Slovakia had never been a truly independent state, and the military has always been associated with foreign (primarily Hungarian) domination. The sense of the military as a tool of foreign powers was sustained during the Communist period when the military was viewed as an arm of Moscow rather than as serving Czechoslovak interests. The Czechoslovak military has no history of defending the state or the government; thus the military cannot point to any historical experience to form a myth that identifies the military with safeguarding national sovereignty.

The military's low prestige has important consequences for Czechoslovak civil-military relations and for Czech national security policy more generally. It affects the willingness of the Czechoslovak people and new civilian leaders to place trust and responsibility in military leaders and military judgments, and limits the role of military forces as an overall part of Czechoslovak national security strategy. It also has an impact on military recruitment, morale, and even combat effectiveness.

Conference discussions showed a high level of awareness of this problem among the Czechoslovak participants. Several Czechoslovak military and civilian commentators stated that defense awareness in Czechoslovakia is negligible. Indeed, one Czechoslovak civilian participant suggested that many Czechoslovak citizens might question whether Czechoslovakia needs a military at all.

Several Czechoslovak participants added concrete insights to this basic problem. For example, a civilian commentator mentioned that the Czechoslovak military's proudest achievements—the exploits of the Czechoslovak Legion during the Russian Civil War and the Czechoslovak units' participation alongside the Allies during World War II—took place outside Czechoslovak territory. His comment suggested that the public could not readily identify those efforts as a substitute for defending the state. He also noted that whenever the uniformed military assumed control of the state (as happened in 1938–39 and 1968), political catastrophe followed. The reference to General Svoboda's presidency in 1968 was a rhetorical one, for the context differed greatly from the events in 1938–39. However, in the view of the Czechoslovak participant, the two events were roughly comparable, and they created severe public image problems for the military. Finally, several civilian participants commented on the post–World War II history of the Czechoslovak military. Czechoslovak armed forces were subordinate to the Communist party and to the USSR. The offensive mission assigned to the Czechoslovak armed forces by the USSR only strengthened public perceptions of the military as a foreign-serving institution. Another Czechoslovak civilian participant added that the military's political indoctrination under the Communists furthered its estrangement from the society. The commentator noted that the military inculcated among conscripts an image of (West) Germany and the United States as the enemy, a view not shared by most of the society.

Czechoslovak participants recognized that the negative perceptions of the military in Czechoslovakia had a deep legacy that would take several decades to erase. A Czechoslovak civilian commentator alluded to the experience in the interwar period as a parallel to the current problem. According to him, military officials in the early years of the first Czechoslovak Republic publicly acknowledged that there was "no other more hated institution" than the military. However, such negative views toward the military changed over a period of 10 to 15 years, and the Czechoslovak participant hoped the same would happen in the new, democratic, post-Communist Czechoslovakia. Several Czechoslovak commentators were mildly optimistic that the change in perceptions already had begun. As one example of a new chapter in Czechoslovak military's history, a Czechoslovak civilian participant pointed to the inclusion of a Czechoslovak unit in the allied forces assembled in the war against Iraq in early 1991. According to him, it was highly significant that the Czechoslovak military acted as a part of a coalition of forces assembled by democratic countries. In his view, the Czechoslovak contribution was a symbolic break with the prior four decades' association of the military with a Communist dictatorship.

In the same vein, a Czechoslovak civilian participant argued that the change toward a greater understanding and support of the armed forces will continue because, in a sovereign Czechoslovakia, the population is beginning to realize that some security risks remain, especially the potential for ethnic strife in the USSR, which might spill over into Czechoslovakia. There is some question as to the validity of such comments. Undoubtedly, fear of spillover of ethnic strife from Ukraine into Slovakia has increased the defense awareness in Slovakia (where the issue has been actively promoted by Slovak ethnic nationalist leaders), but whether the perception has spread to the Czech lands is less certain.

A Czechoslovak military participant added that polls taken in January 1991 showed that the military's popularity had increased, with over 50 percent of respondents approving of the military. A Czechoslovak civilian commentator further dissected the components of the public's attitudes. According to him, the low prestige was attached mainly to the top ranks of the officer corps. The generals and colonels identified closely with the old regime had a much higher disapproval rating than the military as a whole. He cited public opinion polls taken in late 1990 and in May 1991, which showed that while about 50 percent of the respondents expressed confidence in the military as a whole, only some 30 percent expressed confidence in the officer corps. He demonstrated this point even more vividly by citing another poll that measured the perceptions of the youth toward the military as a profession; a professional officer at the rank of a major came in 93rd on a list of desired occupations.

It was clear that most of the Czechoslovak civilian and military participants at the workshop recognized the important role played by the military in safeguarding state sovereignty. None of the workshop participants questioned the necessity of keeping the military. However, they had no illusions about having a long way to go in establishing a truly widespread base of support for the military in Czechoslovakia. They clearly envied the situation in other countries. For example, a Czechoslovak civilian participant commented that the high level of prestige of the military in Poland "took his breath away." Similarly, a Czechoslovak military participant admired the U.S. public's support of the military during the war against Iraq. Although the Czechoslovak participants seemed to realize that the task of increasing the military's esteem was one they had to achieve on their own, a Czechoslovak civilian commentator formulated a specific request to the U.S. participants for advice. In his opinion, Czechoslovakia lacked an organization that would instill a measure of defense awareness among the youth. The organization that performed this task under the old regime (SVAZARM, the Czechoslovak counterpart of the Soviet DOSAAF) had been disbanded, and the successor organization, the Defense Union, had not yet become fully operational. The commentator stated that Czechoslovak officials are still trying to define the role of the Defense Union and are looking for ways to increase young people's awareness of defense issues. The commentator welcomed U.S. advice in this area.

This particular point provides an example of the evolutionary rather than revolutionary change in Czechoslovak thinking on defense preparation. The Czechoslovak official still thought in terms of governmental control—channeled through a specific institution—over the process of developing defense awareness among the youth, rather than relying on an individual's own development of the concept of citizenship to ensure support for the defense of the state.

Perhaps as an indication of the still tense overall relationship between the civilians and the military, the Czechoslovak military participants contributed little to the discussions, and there were only a few differences voiced between the military and civilians on the issue of increasing the prestige of the military. On one occasion, a Czechoslovak military participant questioned whether the new civilian political elite had done enough to integrate the military into the new sovereign Czechoslovakia. In turn, a Czechoslovak civilian participant commented that the military has not been as active as it should be in formulating policies relevant to security matters.

ESTABLISHING PARLIAMENTARY CONTROL OVER THE MILITARY

At the time the workshop took place, the Federal Assembly had established substantial, if still somewhat incomplete, control over the military. To assess how far the changes have actually progressed, it is useful to review the state of affairs prior to the political changes. A Czechoslovak civilian participant described the previous extent of Communist control in some detail. According to him, the Communist party had direct control of the military; the Central Committee of the Czechoslovak Communist party made all the decisions concerning the military in the form of direct orders from the Politburo. A Military Defense Commission within the Central Committee dealt with more detailed tasks and issued guidelines to the Ministry of Defense as to what it was expected to do for the year as well as a timetable to implement the tasks. According to the Czechoslovak representative, this arrangement completely bypassed the state bodies constitutionally empowered to decide these matters—the Office of the President and the Federal Assembly (the two-chamber Czechoslovak parliament)—removing from them any control of the military, while the State Defense Council that was attached to the government played only an auxiliary role.

This arrangement was not a problem as long as top Communist officials also held the top state positions. The situation simply reflected the fact that the Communist party was the locus of power and decision making in Communist Czechoslovakia, and state bodies were just a facade. The ouster of Communists from leadership positions threw the arrangement in turmoil. As the Czechoslovak speaker put it, the task of the new opposition-dominated government that came to power in December 1989 was to transform the system so that the constitutional bodies would actually perform the roles assigned to them.

When the new government was formed, the new leadership perceived the military and the police as posing the biggest internal threats to the consolidation of the political changes. According to a Czechoslovak civilian participant, Vacek soon ameliorated the new government's concerns about the military by offering Havel a gentleman's agreement. In the words of the participant, Vacek told Havel that "you have a great deal of things to worry about, so I wish to offer a guarantee that you will not have to worry about the army." Havel accepted the offer (which must have been made on December 7, 1989, during the first Vacek-Havel meeting), and several Czechoslovak commentators agreed that, in retrospect, the deal had served the country well and that Vacek had played a constructive role. In return, the military implemented a reform program of its own, and was periodically pushed into more vigorous action by the Federal Assembly, while the new government consolidated its position by dealing with the Ministry of Interior (the police) domestically and the withdrawal of Soviet troops from Czechoslovakia in the international sphere.

The police were perceived as a serious threat because of their size and secretiveness. During the two decades that followed the "Prague Spring," the various police force formations in Czechoslovakia had grown enormously. Indeed, it took several weeks for the new authorities in charge of the Ministry of Interior even to begin to understand the myriad secret police organizations and their relationship to each other. Fears of the old guard using the police to destabilize the new government were well founded. A Czechoslovak civilian spokesman stated that the secret police leadership decided on December 12, 1989, not to oppose the new government with violence but to "submerge" and adopt a wait-and-see attitude. The old guard in the internal security apparatus engaged in many attempts to subvert the new government, including embarrassing it by periodically exposing some of the new officials as ex-collaborators and even setting off a bomb in Prague just before the parliamentary elections. The military's constructive role during the crucial period following the political change allowed the new government to concentrate on eliminating the threat from the old guard within the internal security apparatus.

The arrangement between Havel and Vacek came to an end in the fall of 1990. In the words of one Czechoslovak civilian participant, trust has its place in politics, but in September 1990, the time came for a revision of the Havel-Vacek deal, and the Federal Assembly focused its attention seriously on the military. The timing of the move corresponded to the well-advanced reform of the Ministry of Interior, the free election of a new, fully representative parliament, the agreement on Soviet military withdrawal from Czechoslovakia, and increasingly, the open dissension and breakdown within the Warsaw Pact itself.

Several Czechoslovak participants described three components of the process of establishing civilian oversight by the parliament over the military: (1) legislative action, (2) applying budgetary pressure, and (3) setting up of the Office of the General Inspectorate of the Armed Forces. By passing specific laws, the parliament acted to force changes upon the military. For example, the law on military service, adopted in March 1990, allowed alternative service for draftees and created problems with the staffing blueprints developed by the military. The Federal Assembly also discussed several drafts of a new military doctrine (before finally adopting one version in March 1991) that elaborated on the directions of change for the military.

Determining the size of the Defense Ministry's budget has been among the most powerful tools of the new East European parliaments for forcing military responsiveness and accountability. The Defense Ministry's budget was slashed from 33 billion korunas in 1989 to 30.5 billion korunas in 1990 and to 26.5 billion korunas in 1991 (reduced by the Federal Assembly over the military's objections from a proposed 28.5 billion koruna budget), without adjusting for inflation. This represents an enormous drop in the funds appropriated to the military. Because of the need to upgrade salaries (by 50 to 60 percent, according to one Czechoslovak civilian participant) as part of the move toward greater professionalization of the military, there was an unprecedented drop in funds allocated to the Defense Ministry for procurement and operating costs. As a result, as one Czechoslovak military participant put it, funds allocated to the Defense Ministry are now spent in a completely different manner from the way they were spent just two years ago.

The parliament's new control over the budget process contrasts sharply with the state of affairs prior to the political changes. As a Czechoslovak civilian commentator reminded the participants, previously the budget of the Defense Ministry had been camouflaged, with many items hidden in other ministries' budgets. The parliament had no real control over the budget. At the time of the workshop, parliamentary control over the budgetary process already had evolved to include procedures similar to those used in Western democratic countries. According to a Czechoslovak military spokesman, the current process consists of the Ministry of Defense evaluating its needs and goals and then submitting suggestions to the government. In turn, the government evaluates the proposals, modifies them as it deems appropriate, and presents them to the Federal Assembly. The ensuing negotiations within the parliament and between the government and the parliament lead to a compromise draft budget bill that is then voted on by the Federal Assembly.

One Czechoslovak civilian representative felt that the Federal Assembly had made great strides in gaining oversight of the military through the budget process, but he added that a few shortcomings remained. The commentator stated that the Federal Assembly still had no budgetary oversight of military secret services (presumably, military intelligence and military counterintelligence). The spokesman compared the situation unfavorably with that in Germany, where closed parliamentary committees composed of selected members of the various parties and factions review the military secret services' operations. The Czechoslovak representative specifically asked for the advice and assistance of the U.S. Congress in setting up a structure for the Czechoslovak parliament's oversight of the military's intelligence bodies.

The General Inspectorate has been a contentious issue in civil-military relations since the political changes. Members of the new political elite have pressed for setting up an oversight body subordinate only to the Federal Assembly, which would in effect bypass the Ministry of Defense in overseeing military reforms. Not surprisingly, the top ranks of the military had resisted creating such an organization. In the words of one Czechoslovak civilian participant, the bill setting up a General Inspectorate has been the subject of a lengthy, behind-the-scenes struggle. The military leadership has called the proposed General Inspectorate redundant and claimed that it would complicate the division of power over the military between the President and the Federal Assembly. The Czechoslovak commentator felt that the military perceived direct and strict parliamentary supervision as threatening since it was accustomed only to political controls. The commentator thought that such views predominated among the upper ranks but they were not shared by junior officers. The participant had held extensive conversations with junior officers (most under 40 years old) throughout Czechoslovakia, and he felt they supported setting up a General Inspectorate as soon as possible.

Shortly before the workshop took place, the formation of the General Inspectorate had been approved. A Czechoslovak civilian participant explained its future structure and role. According to him, the Office of the General Inspectorate was to have a general inspector, a deputy general inspector, and 17 inspectors. The main staff of the General Inspectorate was to be composed of specialists in specific fields (management, economics, humanitarian affairs, etc.), to be elected by the Federal Assembly, and to be accountable only to the Assembly. The commentator expected that the body would regularly report to the Presidium and the Defense and Security Committee of the Federal Assembly.

Many discussions at the workshop centered on the U.S. model of civil-military relations. This topic was of great interest to the Czechoslovak participants, some of whom were directly engaged in setting up or modifying the country's institutions. Although the U.S. model offers lessons for Czechoslovakia, several U.S. participants emphasized that U.S. institutions reflected the unique character of U.S. history and political culture. As such, these institutions work well, but Czechoslovak participants were cautioned against blindly copying the U.S. model. U.S. participants did stress, however, that whatever specific approaches Czechoslovakia chooses to adopt, the basic principle of direct civilian oversight of the military was worth retaining.

CURTAILING COMMUNIST INFLUENCE WITHIN THE MILITARY

In parallel with increased parliamentary control over the Czechoslovak military, the Czechoslovak government has acted to change old mechanisms of Communist party control of the military and to eliminate sources of Communist influence within the armed forces so as to transform the military into a genuine state-serving institution. Under the old regime, in Czechoslovakia as well as in other East European countries, the Main Political Administration (MPA) of the Armed Forces and the party's political apparatus within the military served as the overt vehicles of party control over the military. They were supplemented by a covert vehicle, the military counterintelligence organization, which was subordinated to the civilian internal security organization and in fact constituted an arm of the police (like the KGB control of the Soviet military). Widespread Communist party membership of the officer corps (compulsory at higher ranks) aimed to co-opt the officers to the regime.

This arrangement was obviously unacceptable after the revolution. Soon after the political changes, the pillars of Communist supervision of the military began to be toppled. The Main Political Administration and the system of party cells within the military were the first to go. A reorganization of military counterintelligence followed. An extensive process of screening every officer for loyalty also began, with most attention devoted to the upper ranks of the officer corps. The whole process was administered largely by Vacek, but by the fall of 1990, the parliament had raised objections to what it termed an incomplete and slow process of military reform. Dobrovsky ordered a reinvestigation of the officer screening process and pressed forward with restructuring military counterintelligence. Shortly before the beginning of the workshop, most of the results of the initial screening investigation were upheld, and a new military counterintelligence organization began to function.

Although MPA and primary party cells within the military were abolished in December 1989, many ex-MPA officers continued to work in the Education and Culture Administration, a body that was set up following the abolition of the MPA. The media widely criticized the new body as the MPA in a new form, despite the vehement objections (echoed by several Czechoslovak civilian participants at the workshop) that the new body was not a continuation of the MPA. The Education and Culture Administration was restructured in late 1990 and renamed the Social Management Administration. According to a Czechoslovak civilian participant, the new body's goals entailed the "cultivation of human potential skills." He claimed that the personnel from the Social Management Administration are social scientists who provide expert advice to commanders. As the spokesman emphasized, the system is not a continuation of the old system of dual control of a unit (by a line commander and a political officer).

There is some rationale for such officers in the Czechoslovak military because the political officers had been responsible for social welfare of the soldiers. Line commanders were not trained in such tasks. Nevertheless, in the long run, an intra-military department whose tasks include the "patriotic upbringing" of the conscripts seemed unnecessary to some of the U.S. participants. Its continued presence in the Czechoslovak military represents another example of the lack of a complete break with past practices.

Military counterintelligence presented a special problem. The organization was thoroughly penetrated by the KGB, and according to one Czechoslovak civilian participant, it had been converted into an instrument serving Soviet security interests as early as 1951. Military counterintelligence had been subordinated to the Ministry of Interior (controlled by that Ministry's 10th Department, according to the commentator) and given the task of combating the ideological "internal enemy." Thus, while every military needs a counterintelligence organization, the new Czechoslovak government had to change theirs fundamentally so that it would no longer spy on line officers but instead focus on upholding security guidelines within the Czechoslovak military.

According to a Czechoslovak civilian commentator, the commission that carried out the second detailed screening of military counterintelligence personnel (following Dobrovsky's appointment) examined all available evidence regarding its staff, including some 7,000 letters received from military personnel and civilians. The commentator added that the dislike of the military counterintelligence personnel had been so great and the refusal to work with them so widespread that the commission originally envisioned retaining only 70 members of the old organization. Since that number proved too low, the reorganized and renamed military counterintelligence organization ended up with 117 members who had been on the staff of the old body. In addition, a much larger military police force was formed (no such organization had existed previously).

The Czechoslovak media have criticized retaining any members of the old military counterintelligence. However, if the discussions in the Federal Assembly are taken as a sign, the small size of the new organization, the strict screening process, the retention of so few staff members, and the institutional subordination of the new military counterintelligence service directly to the Minister of Defense have removed some of the worries regarding the loyalty of the body and its potential for misuse. Once the Federal Assembly achieves direct oversight of military counterintelligence, any residual fears should diminish further.

The policy of retaining many officers who had been members of the Communist party also came under much media and some parliamentary criticism in 1990. The Czechoslovak media often portrayed the policy as misguided and an example of partial reform that failed to go to the root of the problem. A Czechoslovak civilian participant defended the policy by contrasting the two possible approaches to reform: a "radical" and a "thinning" approach. The radical approach would require replacing all commanders (94 percent of whom had been Communist party members, according to him). The commentator dismissed this view as naive. In his opinion, this approach would destabilize the military. The thinning approach that was adopted involved an extensive screening process designed to place blame where it belonged instead of punishing all officers on the principle of collective guilt.

The Federal Assembly also outlawed all political activity in the military, including soldiers' membership in political parties. This move infringed upon the personal liberties of soldiers as citizens and it caused some dissatisfaction in the military. A Czechoslovak civilian commentator defended the action on the grounds that the overwhelming majority of officers had been members of the Communist party and the move aimed to eliminate the risk that the military might become an arena of political struggle. The commentator added that, in the future, the Bundeswehr will be the model for relations between the military and political parties in Czechoslovakia. It is unclear as to what the commentator was specifically referring; presumably, he envisioned a military operating under democratic military statutes, accepting civilian control, committed to the defense of parliamentary democracy, and with members of parliament from any party having the right to contribute to deliberations regarding the armed forces.

The spokesman further noted that the Free Legion (a group of non-Communist officers who campaigned actively in favor of the radical approach to the problem of Communist or ex-Communist officers in the military) had attempted to repoliticize the military by establishing contacts with the People's Party (a right-wing nationalist group), though he claimed the effort was unsuccessful. The Free Legion was a topic of some embarrassment to the Czechoslovak participants associated with the military. One Czechoslovak military spokesman dismissed the Free Legion as a small "interest group" operating outside the military and without much of a base of support. While the group had been prominent in the summer and fall of 1990 (and played a role in driving Vacek from office), it has since lost some of its appeal. Nevertheless, the very existence of such a group would be a cause of concern to any military, for it indicates a deep split within the officer corps, and it is undoubtedly a thorn in the side of the Czechoslovak military.

Dobrovsky's review of the officer screening process failed to turn up any significant shortcomings. A Czechoslovak military participant strongly emphasized that the reattestation upheld the view that the Czechoslovak officer corps was composed of highly capable military experts who felt a sense of strong responsibility and allegiance to their homeland, though, as a result of long-standing and strong political pressures, their capability for independent political thinking had been "reduced." The verification process did lead to some reshuffling of personnel at the highest posts. For example, a new Chief of the General Staff was appointed a few weeks before the workshop took place. In addition, there has been an influx of officers who had been purged after 1968. Many of these officers have taken up influential posts in the military.

The discussions concerning the staffing needs of the Czechoslovak military led to presenting some specific requests to the U.S. participants. One Czechoslovak civilian participant bluntly asserted that "the major contribution through which you can help is to assist us in training and educating new officers." The request envisions assistance at the junior and middle officer level (captain and major). According to the commentator, 66 Czechoslovak officers were still being trained in the USSR (mostly in technical specialties), though such cooperation was rapidly decreasing. As these officers finish their studies, their number is expected to drop drastically (down to eight in 1992, according to the participant), in keeping with the expressed wish of Czechoslovak officials to cut such ties or limit them to a minimum. A Czechoslovak military participant differed a bit, claiming that because the Czechoslovak military still relies on Soviet-made armaments, a few Czechoslovak officers probably will continue to be trained in the USSR. In any event, Czechoslovak participants unanimously agreed on the importance of cooperating with the United States in the sphere of officer training.

RESTRUCTURING THE MINISTRY OF DEFENSE

The role of the Ministry of Defense in Communist Czechoslovakia (and in other Warsaw Pact countries) differed substantially from the role of such ministries in Western democratic countries. Indeed, the military in Czechoslovakia was accountable only to the Soviet regime and the Soviet military, with the Czechoslovak Communist party (dependent on the USSR to stay in power) playing a supervisory role for the Soviets. This arrangement eliminated the need for any formal distinction between troop command and the civilian Ministry, since Czechoslovak state bodies played no real role anyway. Because the military was not in fact accountable to state bodies, it had a complete monopoly on all matters pertaining to defense, and uniformed military staffed all important posts within the Ministry.

The new Czechoslovak government faced the task of fundamentally restructuring the Ministry of Defense. They began with such matters as formally establishing the scope and extent of the Ministry's responsibilities. The most important reform has been the separation of functions between the political-administrative activities performed increasingly by civilians at the Ministry of Defense and the command of the troops carried out by the General Staff. The conceptual underpinnings for the reform had been worked out while Vacek was still in charge of the Defense Ministry. According to one Czechoslovak civilian participant, the preparations involved many discussions and clashes with some of the military figures then in high positions within the Ministry. The program began to be implemented soon after Dobrovsky's appointment as Minister of Defense, and, in April 1991, the reformed Ministry of Defense consisted of three main departments: (1) Strategic Planning, (2) Economic Management, and (3) Social and Humanitarian Affairs. The Minister of Defense is personally responsible for personnel administration (which includes formulating concepts governing personnel policies), the inspection department, and military courts. The chiefs of the three main departments are also Deputy Defense Ministers. Together with the Chief of the General Staff (also a Deputy Defense Minister), they form a supreme advisory body to the Defense Minister. According to a Czechoslovak civilian participant, the role of this advisory body is to resolve main strategic and conceptual questions.

A Czechoslovak civilian participant provided some insights into the extent of the changes required. For example, all matters relating to strategic planning previously had been "drafted by Moscow." Now the new leadership had to start from scratch to develop truly Czechoslovak national security doctrine, operational goals, and programs, issues that had not been dealt with for over 40 years.

At the time of the workshop, the precise roles of the various subsections within the Ministry of Defense were still being worked out. For example, during the workshop, a Czechoslovak military participant was interrupted to resolve the issue of whether the scientific and technological development division (part of Strategic Planning) was to report directly to the Minister of Defense or whether the General Staff would have some supervisory authority. The specific functions of the Economic Management department also seemed to be in a state of flux, due to the transition from a planned to a market economy and the consequent transformation of the military's role in the economy.

There is a civilian presence at the Ministry of Defense beginning with the Minister and the Deputy Defense Minister in charge of Social and Humanitarian Affairs. There is no set policy on how many of the Deputy Defense Ministers (four altogether) are to be civilians, though at least one slot seems to be reserved for the military, since the Chief of Staff is automatically also a Deputy Defense Minister. A Czechoslovak civilian participant stated that many intermediate posts within the Ministry of Defense are also staffed by civilians. The civilians are especially visible in the Social and Humanitarian Affairs department. The department includes the controversial Social Management Administration, but its responsibilities include the whole sphere of human resources in the military. According to a Czechoslovak civilian commentator, the department concentrates on everything related to educational and social policies within the military, and it is becoming an important organization for improving relations between soldiers by providing sociological research services and psychological expertise. The influx of civilians into the Ministry of Defense represents a profound change, for in the words of a Czechoslovak military participant, "the military had been accustomed to a purely military staff within the Ministry."

The initial assignment of a major part of the troop command to the General Staff was to have been completed on October 1, 1991 (and it seems to have taken place). A Czechoslovak military participant stated that in working out the conceptual underpinnings of military reform, Czechoslovak officials have been guided by the experiences of the Western militaries (especially the U.S. Army), though, in the case of the finer points concerning the separation of tasks between the Ministry of Defense and the General Staff, the Italian model proved especially useful. It is unclear what the reference to the Italian model meant, since Italy provides a fairly standard Western example of division of tasks between the Ministry of Defense and the General Staff.

That Czechoslovak officials have been influenced by Western ideas is hardly a secret, but it was interesting to note the degree to which Czechoslovak participants are familiar with contemporary U.S. intellectual currents. For example, one Czechoslovak civilian spokesman explained that Peter Drucker's ideas on management have provided the basic philosophy for transforming the Ministry of Defense. Czechoslovak participants expressed interest in the possibility of training Czechoslovak military and civilians at U.S. schools of management. According to a Czechoslovak civilian participant, a management school for defense personnel has been set up in Czechoslovakia, and Czechoslovak officials have been in close contact with similar centers in Sweden and Germany. In this context, the commentator welcomed the extension of the U.S. IMET (International Military Education and Training) program to Czechoslovakia and expressed hopes for greater cooperation in the future. On a somewhat sarcastic note, a Czechoslovak military participant suggested that it might be possible to improve the "less-than-best" quality of civilians dealing with strategic matters in Czechoslovakia by educating a greater number of them in strategic studies programs at Western universities or institutes.

ETHNIC CONFLICT

The Czech-Slovak ethnic conflict emerged immediately following the old regime's ouster, and it has evolved to a point where there is real doubt as to whether Czechoslovakia will survive as a state. The conflict stems from a widely shared Slovak perception that Czechs discriminate against the Slovaks. The conflict permeates virtually all political issues in Czechoslovakia. Although opinion polls show that the majority of Slovaks still favor some form of association with the Czechs, the intensity of Slovak ethnic nationalism may block any compromise. The dissolution of Yugoslavia and the breakup of the USSR could hasten similar developments in Czechoslovakia.

The Czech-Slovak issue has been complicated by the rise of regionalist assertiveness. The Moravian and Silesian movement for autonomy has been spectacularly successful, leading toward the assertion of a separate Moravian and Silesian ethnic identity, and it has caused a split in the Czech lands. In addition, Slovakia contains a number of non-Slovak ethnic groups, and the rise of militant Slovak nationalism has exacerbated relations between Slovaks and the large Hungarian minority in southern Slovakia. Ruthenians and Ukrainians, concentrated in eastern Slovakia, also have shown signs of ethnic mobilization. The pockets of Germans and Poles (mainly in the Czech lands) have remained largely quiet, but their attitude may change if the Czechoslovak state begins to disintegrate. Indeed, in early 1992, ethnic Poles showed signs of ethnic assertiveness. Finally, the Romanies (Gypsies), for years the target of discriminatory policies, have begun to organize along ethnic lines.

Conference discussions largely avoided the issue of ethnic conflict, though the matter was always in the background. For example, one participant alluded to discriminatory practices and Czech domination of Czechoslovakia by expressing regrets that he had to make his comments in Czech rather than in his native language. Similarly, a sharp exchange between Czechoslovak participants ensued regarding Slovakia's previous attempts at statehood.

A Czechoslovak civilian commentator reminded the participants of the smaller ethnic groups that inhabited the country. In this connection, he seemed distrustful of the effect that granting greater powers to the republican (i.e., Slovak) bodies would have on the functioning of the defense councils at the local level (each district in Czechoslovakia had a defense council as part of the mobilization and territorial defense structure). He felt that there was a need to ensure that the defense councils at the local level would be staffed by officials from the region rather than from republican administrative bodies. The comments were clearly made in connection with the Hungarian minority in Slovakia, and they were motivated by the fear that Slovaks would obtain a greater say in matters affecting Hungarians at the local level. Despite the fact that a U.S. civilian commentator also touched on the topic, other Czechoslovak participants did not address the issue. Similarly, even though the U.S. participant alluded to the demands for forming a Slovak territorial militia (the Home Guard), Czechoslovak participants failed to comment on the topic (though it is of critical importance).

The one ethnic issue addressed directly at the workshop concerned a Slovak ethnic nationalist soldiers' group, the Association of Slovak Soldiers (or ASV in its Slovak acronym). The group was set up in January 1991, and it has openly advocated forming a separate Slovak army. Another less militant Slovak ethnic nationalist group of soldiers—the Stefanik Legion—was set up a short time later. A Czechoslovak military participant objected to the phrasing of a U.S. civilian commentator who referred to ASV as a group "within the army." He dismissed ASV in the same terms as the Free Legion, namely, a relatively small but noisy "interest group" that is composed of soldiers but operates outside the military. A Czechoslovak civilian participant noted the ties between ASV and the Slovak National Party (a major source of expression of Slovak ethnic nationalist sentiments), but he also dismissed the group as having "weak influence."

These views seem too optimistic in view of the ever-increasing level of ethnic conflict in Czechoslovakia. If anything, the emergence of ASV shows that the ethnic conflict has spread to the military. Ethnic conflict is bound to have a divisive influence on the military, and it will have a damaging effect on the functioning, efficiency, and cohesion of the Czechoslovak armed forces. In any event, a single Czechoslovak military is far from assured since the continuity of the unified state is increasingly in doubt.

3. NATIONAL SECURITY POLICY

INTRODUCTION

The principal goals of the Czechoslovak revolution—establishing a liberal democracy and a market economy—represent an unambiguous commitment to Western political and economic values. For both symbolic and practical reasons, the new Czechoslovak government has focused on integrating the nation with Western political organizations and economic structures, and distancing Czechoslovakia from its old links to the Soviet Union, especially the political and security links through the Warsaw Pact.

The first concrete goal of Czechoslovak national security policy was to secure the rapid withdrawal of Soviet troops. Removing the Soviet troops not only symbolized the rupture with the old regime, it also represented an important guarantee against a change in Soviet policy that might seek to restore Soviet influence. The treaty legitimating the Soviet troop presence had been signed in the aftermath of the August 1968 Soviet-led invasion. The new Czechoslovak officials immediately asserted that because the treaty was imposed on Czechoslovakia, it was invalid under international law. On December 8, 1990, the Czechoslovak Foreign Minister presented a note to Soviet officials asking that talks begin on the full withdrawal of Soviet troops in the shortest possible time. The issue at once became a central question in Czechoslovak-Soviet relations.

Negotiations on full Soviet withdrawal started in mid-January 1990 and, following President Havel's visit to Moscow, an agreement was signed on February 26, 1990. It stipulated full withdrawal by June 30, 1991, a compromise from the initial Czechoslovak proposal that all Soviet troops leave by the end of 1990. The Soviet military seemed to have been taken by surprise by the demand for a rapid and complete withdrawal. Initially, the Soviets thought only in terms of establishing a new legal basis for their presence in Czechoslovakia and wanted to link any withdrawal to the then ongoing disarmament talks in Vienna.

Despite continuing disputes over compensation (the Soviets wanted Czechoslovakia to pay for buildings and facilities left behind; the Czechoslovaks sought Soviet compensation for environmental damage and clean-up costs) the withdrawal proceeded as scheduled. By the time the workshop was held, most Soviet troops had departed.

More broadly, the Czechoslovak government (like its East European neighbors) had to grapple with the question of the Warsaw Pact's future. The underlying Czechoslovak goal was withdrawal from the Warsaw Pact. In order not to provoke the Soviet Union, Czechoslovak officials asserted that Czechoslovakia did not intend to leave the Pact unilaterally and might contemplate retaining the Pact as a political alliance of fully independent nations without a military component (a course also proposed by Polish officials, who saw a political alliance as a possible counterweight and bargaining chip with Germany during the controversy over the Polish-German border during the process of German unification). The Czechoslovak approach thus differed from the strategy advocated by many Hungarian officials and parliamentarians, who called for Hungary's immediate withdrawal from the Pact; indeed Havel explicitly distanced himself from the Hungarian discussions. But fundamental tensions between the East Europeans and the Soviets, particularly over unified Germany's membership in NATO, soon led Czechoslovak officials to conclude that completing the conventional arms control treaty in Europe was the only remaining useful role for the Warsaw Pact.

Nonetheless, the actual winding up of the Pact went slowly. Until June 1990, Czechoslovak officials took few concrete steps to alter the Pact. But, as Havel himself noted, the June 1990 Warsaw Pact Political Consultative Committee meeting in Moscow was a turning point. It resulted in a plan for a far-reaching transformation of the Pact and a timetable to achieve it. Czechoslovak officials proposed deemphasizing the military aspects of the Warsaw Pact and removing direct Warsaw Pact (thus, Soviet) control over the non-Soviet Warsaw Pact armies. The goal was to transform the Warsaw Pact into a loose coalition that would serve as little more than a negotiating vehicle for arms reductions, and to permit de jure resubordination of non-Soviet Warsaw Pact armed forces to their respective national commands.

The Warsaw Pact members set up a commission to work out these steps, with non-Soviet Warsaw Pact members expecting to implement them by November 1990. Top Czechoslovak officials, including the Prime Minister, made Czechoslovak membership in the Warsaw Pact conditional on such a transformation, underlining that the Czechoslovak armed forces would be subordinated solely to national (rather than Warsaw Pact) command by December 1990. The commission met several times in the summer of 1990, but its aim of transforming the Warsaw Pact became increasingly pointless, as the Pact was already collapsing. Hungary made withdrawal from the Pact its official policy, and, by October 1990, the diverging interests between the East Europeans and the USSR on arms control, exacerbated by

Soviet military intransigence against meaningful transformation of the Pact, effectively put an end to efforts to maintain even the facade of an alliance. The Warsaw Pact was formally dissolved on July 1, 1991.

The Czechoslovak effort to transform, and ultimately to dissolve, the Warsaw Pact was a component of its broader strategy to replace both Cold War blocs (NATO and the Warsaw Pact) with a pan-European collective security system. Havel and Dienstbier believed that the Conference on Security and Cooperation in Europe (CSCE) process could be transformed rapidly into a new security framework that would replace East-West divisions and meet the security needs of both Eastern Europe and the Soviet Union. In early 1990, Havel called for the withdrawal of U.S. troops from Europe, and Dienstbier sent a memorandum to the 35 CSCE nations calling for the creation of a "European Security Commission." The Czechoslovak approach held some appeal for the USSR, which was searching for a formulation that would preclude a unified Germany from remaining in NATO.

As disputes with the USSR over Soviet troop withdrawals and the future of the Pact continued through 1990, however, the Czechoslovak government began to shift its views on European security arrangements. While clinging to the long-term goal of a European collective security arrangement (a second Dienstbier memo was issued in the Spring of 1991, along with a joint Czechoslovak-German foreign ministers' declaration embracing the concept), Czechoslovakia moved closer to NATO. Czechoslovak officials ceased calling for disbanding NATO and instead began to stress NATO's importance as a pillar for the future CSCE framework of European security (without according the Warsaw Pact a similar role). Officials also rejected neutrality, since neutrality would keep Czechoslovakia out of military alliances such as NATO in the future. Czechoslovak officials feared that proposals for a neutral Central/Eastern Europe would leave Czechoslovakia exposed to Soviet political and military pressure, and similarly rejected the idea of a regional alliance as an inadequate substitute for Western ties (although in March 1991 the leaders of Poland, Czechoslovakia, and Hungary, meeting in Visegrad, Hungary, did agree to enhance regional cooperation, including security policy).

Spurred by NATO Secretary General Manfred Woerner's trip to Czechoslovakia in September 1990, Czechoslovak ties with NATO progressively became institutionalized. By the spring of 1991, Czechoslovak officials made no secret of the fact that they hoped to join NATO, although they avoided explicitly applying for membership because NATO made clear (most dramatically in Woerner's remarks to a Czechoslovak-NATO conference in Prague in April 1991) that NATO was unprepared to admit Czechoslovakia. The new, pro-NATO orientation was accompanied by a broad-ranging effort to strengthen relations with the West as a whole. The effort focused primarily on bilateral relations with Germany and the United States, and an accelerated move to enhance Czechoslovakia's ties with the European Community. In March 1991, Czechoslovakia officially adopted a new defensive military doctrine that stipulated the redeployment of Czechoslovak armed forces away from their anti-NATO orientation and toward a declared goal of territorial defense of the entire country.

FOREIGN POLICY

At the time of the workshop, Czechoslovak foreign policy centered around developing close political, security, and economic ties with the West. The last Soviet troops were withdrawing from Czechoslovakia, and Soviet-Czechoslovak relations in all spheres, including security, were under extreme strain. The Czechoslovak government was also seeking to build better relations with Poland and Hungary, after an initial reluctance stemming from fears that regional cooperation would be seen as a substitute for links to the West. Czechoslovak officials had not abandoned their strong support for the CSCE process, though their views had matured toward more realistic expectations.

A Czechoslovak civilian participant divided the Czechoslovak government foreign policy evolution since the Communists' ouster into two main periods. He termed the first period the "romantic approach," stemming from the initial euphoria over communism's collapse in Eastern Europe. The period since the initial euphoria waned, which he referred to as a "more sober and realistic period," was based on the recognition that although the Cold War had ended, great powers remained and their interests had to be respected.

The commentator also listed four basic factors that, in his view, determined the direction of Czechoslovak foreign policy since the ouster of the old regime: (1) failure of previous alliances to guarantee Czechoslovak security (the Munich "sellout" was a notable example); (2) the danger posed by instability in the USSR; (3) German unification and its integration into Western security structures; and (4) ethnic and national conflict in Eastern Europe. In the commentator's view, with the end of the East-West division of Europe, there are no institutions capable of addressing these four areas of concern; a new, all-European collective security system based on institutionalizing the CSCE could best cope with these potential risks to Czechoslovak security.

Polish officials developed a similar approach because they faced similar problems, and the two countries quickly began to cooperate in proposing concrete steps to institutionalize the CSCE. In the commentator's view, the CSCE institutions set up so far, such as the CSCE Secretariat in Prague, the Center for Conflict Prevention in Vienna, and the Office of Free Elections in Warsaw, are important steps in this direction.

Czechoslovak participants shared the view that further institutionalization of the CSCE process and incorporating Czechoslovakia into a wider European security system remained the only available option for Czechoslovakia to guarantee its security in the long run. A Czechoslovak civilian commentator explained why other options did not seem viable: A formal alliance of Central East European states was unacceptable because the USSR would perceive such an arrangement as hostile to its interests, and East Europeans continued to see a need to treat Soviet security interests gingerly. According to the commentator, there has been great progress in furthering the trilateral cooperation since the three countries' summit in Visegrad in March 1991; the three countries have been coordinating their diplomatic and political moves on a variety of issues. However, several Czechoslovak commentators pointed out that the trilateral cooperation does not contain any formal military component. A U.S. civilian commentator's suggestion that Poland, Czechoslovakia, and Hungary might strengthen their cooperation in areas such as air defense prompted no reply from the Czechoslovak participants. The views expressed by Czechoslovak participants regarding the influence of the USSR in Eastern Europe have changed since the failed coup in Moscow in August 1991 and the consequent collapse of the USSR. Closer ties with Poland and Hungary in the realm of defense have become a reality, and fears of Soviet influence have calmed.

A Czechoslovak civilian rejected the idea, proposed by Henry Kissinger in July 1990, of a Central European neutral bloc consisting of Poland, Czechoslovakia, Hungary, and Austria, because that approach reflected Cold War era thinking. In the participant's view, the concept of neutrality made sense only in the context of continued superpower competition, and was no longer applicable in the post–Cold War era. To illustrate the impact of ongoing European political changes, the commentator cited Austria as a case of a previously neutral country seeking closer ties with EC and NATO. He rejected the notion of transforming the region into a *new cordon sanitaire* or a buffer zone. Although public opinion polls in Czechoslovakia consistently demonstrate strong support for the concept of neutrality, the Czechoslovak participant stressed that it would have to be "neutrality of a different type" (meaning active engagement with other states and suprastate actors rather than isolationism) for it to be adopted by the government. There was no dissent on this analysis; several U.S. participants agreed that the concept of a "gray zone" was not useful for thinking about security in the region. Czechoslovak thinking on the point of neutrality of any kind has changed since the workshop, as the collapse of the USSR has made the whole point moot.

Finally, a Czechoslovak civilian also noted that the option of joining NATO appeared closed to Czechoslovakia. Havel had raised the issue of some form of association of Czechoslovakia with NATO during his visit to NATO headquarters in March 1991, but "unfortunately, even the hope of limited association failed" (Czechoslovak officials knew that NATO would not extend full membership). Showing thinly disguised disappointment, another Czechoslovak civilian participant added that NATO is a closed community that has so far pursued exclusionary policies. Since neither an East Central European security alliance, nor neutrality, nor membership in a Western security organization seemed viable, Czechoslovak participants seemed resigned to the fact that the CSCE remained the only path open to them. That view seems to have been modified since the creation of the North Atlantic Cooperation Council and the ever-increasing ties between the NATO countries and the states of Eastern Europe.

Several U.S. participants emphasized that the rebuff by NATO in March 1991 was not the last word. As one U.S. civilian commentator put it, the process is what is crucial; in May 1990, any talk of NATO ties with Eastern Europe seemed unrealistic, but cooperation has already begun in some spheres and more is envisioned. U.S. commentators suggested that the three Central East European countries will in the long run have the option of joining a West European security organization that has links with the United States. U.S. participants supported this development. One U.S. civilian even suggested that, ultimately, tables will be turned, and that West Europe will actively seek to bring about East European NATO membership as part of a strategy to bring stability and peace to Europe at a lower cost. An American civilian spokesman offered a specific model of steps to take during the current stage of closer but informal NATO-Czechoslovak relations that would bring the two sides closer together. He felt that the examples of NATO cooperation with Sweden during the Cold War and Yugoslavia during the early 1950s offered a useful example of how NATO could build ties with countries with which it had a security interest but where time or circumstances precluded membership. He suggested that the parallel is not exact, but these previous experiences may offer some lessons. It was in this context that he suggested that Czechoslovakia attempt to establish a network of bilateral relationships regarding military aspects of security with Western countries (including the United States). The U.S. participants' comments also seem to have been overtaken by events.

The exchange regarding NATO sparked a comment that poignantly illustrated the Czechoslovak security dilemma. A Czechoslovak civilian participant acknowledged that integrating Czechoslovakia into Western security structures is a process. Because Czechoslovakia is a subject of that process, Czechoslovak officials prefer not to be passive but instead to take an active part in advancing that process. He emphasized the importance of CSCE to Czechoslovakia because of its trans-Atlantic link as well as its more concrete role in enhancing security by solving regional conflicts (for Czechoslovak officials do not expect a continental war). He offered the example of a spillover of a possible civil war in Yugoslavia as one potential opportunity for the CSCE to impose military force to control the conflict.

Czechoslovak participants reacted strongly against John Mearsheimer's thesis that, on grounds of stability, the Cold War division of Europe (buttressed by nuclear deterrence) was preferable to the new multipolar Europe, which was likely to lead to endemic conflict.[1] A Czechoslovak civilian commentator expressed a widely shared reaction by contrasting the different implications of the Cold War for citizens of Western and Eastern Europe. In his view, in the West, the Cold War arrangements provided security, but in Eastern Europe they meant "Sovietization and economic, political, moral, and ethical decay." In the view of East Europeans, the Soviet domination of the region by force was inherently destabilizing and thus created a security problem. The critique implicitly expressed some East Europeans' grievance toward Western security experts who ignore the natural aspirations of East Europeans for self-determination, as well

---

[1]John J. Mearsheimer, "Back to the Future: Instability in Europe after the Cold War," *International Security*, Vol. 15, No. 1, Summer 1990, pp. 5–56. Mearsheimer's argument has also sparked controversy in the United States. For example, see the correspondence by Stanley Hoffman, Robert O. Keohane, Bruce M. Russett, and Thomas Risse-Kappen and Mearsheimer's replies to them. "Back to the Future, Part II: International Relations Theory and Post-Cold War Europe," *International Security*, Vol. 15, No. 2, Fall 1990, pp. 191–199; "Back to the Future, Part III: Realism and the Realities of European Security," *International Security*, Vol. 15, No. 3, Winter 1990–91, pp. 216–222.

as some Westerners' apparent lack of understanding of the connection between domestic and international stability.

Another Czechoslovak civilian participant expanded on this critique. In his view, history does not repeat itself, and suggesting that the European security environment was reverting to a situation similar to 1919 was misguided. Instead, the new more fluid situation illustrated the need for setting up a European-wide security system linked to North America. According to this participant, the foundation of such a system should be NATO, since NATO seemed to be the only current alliance capable of action.

A discussion of the future security risks in Europe indicated that U.S. and Czechoslovak participants generally agreed on the causes of potential instability. A U.S. civilian cautioned that the current security arrangement in Europe was very uncertain. In his view, a security structure held together by the United States was unstable in the long run because the continued U.S. presence in Europe was an anomaly and perhaps not sustainable. Yet the commentator saw no substitute for the U.S. role in ensuring European security. He foresaw no viable European security organization emerging because of competition between France, Great Britain, and Germany. To make the situation even more unbalanced, Germany, the most powerful country in Europe, has no nuclear weapons, has most of the U.S. troops in Europe on its soil, and has an uncertain future foreign policy orientation because of the absorption of the German Democratic Republic (GDR). It seemed entirely feasible to the U.S. commentator that a rift in U.S.-German relations similar to that in current U.S.-Japanese relations might occur, contributing to the departure of U.S. troops from Germany.

Many of these fears regarding Germany were shared by Czechoslovak participants. When a U.S. civilian participant suggested metaphorically that his German interlocutors seem to have grown 20 centimeters taller during 1990, a Czechoslovak civilian commentator responded that, for him, his German colleagues seemed to have grown one meter. In his view, German-Czechoslovak relations are in a trial period, with the treaty between the two countries (initialed in late 1991 and signed in early 1992) bound to have a major influence over the future relations between the two countries. Yet his overall prognosis was positive—a future of extensive and good ties, presumably for reasons of proximity and mutual benefit.

U.S. and Czechoslovak participants differed over the future role of the USSR. A Czechoslovak civilian commentator stated that even without the Baltic republics, Moldova, and Georgia, the Soviet Union (which had still existed at the time of the conference) should not be discounted as a major actor in world politics. He thought it better to integrate the USSR into a new European order and develop a modus vivendi with it rather than isolate it. A healthy respect for Soviet interests in Eastern Europe seems to have motivated his remarks. For example, to illustrate that the Soviets have not given up their perception of Eastern Europe as a special security concern, he noted that a high-ranking Soviet official recently told him that the countries of Eastern Europe will have to cooperate in the future with the USSR in economic, political, and ultimately security fields. Of course, the events in the former USSR since the failed coup attempt have rendered some of these projections obsolete.

MILITARY ISSUES

The adoption of a new Czechoslovak military doctrine in spring 1991 was the culmination of an 18-month process. A key issue concerned the relation of Czechoslovak strategy to its Warsaw Pact allies. The document finally adopted made no reference to any alliance obligations (despite the fact that the Warsaw Pact was officially still in existence at that time), and it envisioned an "all around" territorial defense, using only Czechoslovak resources.

A Czechoslovak military commentator gave some idea of the extent of change by discussing the Czechoslovak military doctrine as it existed prior to the political changes in November 1989. According to him, Czechoslovakia had a satellite military doctrine imposed by the Soviet Union; the doctrine simply reflected Soviet interests, and it had many negative consequences for Czechoslovakia, some of which are felt keenly to this day. Czechoslovak forces had been assigned an offensive mission that would take them into southern West Germany. The equipment and command and communications structure used by the Czechoslovak military corresponded to these goals. In addition, the industrial and mobilizational structure reflected the Soviet strategic objectives. Referring to the Slovak refusal to accept the federal Czechoslovak decision to convert the Slovak armaments industry to civilian production (because the program would cause enormous economic dislocation), several Czechoslovak military spokesmen emphasized that locating much of the Czechoslovak armaments industry in Slovakia (and away from the previous "strategic enemy," West Germany) was one of the consequences of the previous subordination to the Soviet Union. One commentator warned that the United States should watch the level of tension caused by economic problems in Czechoslovakia. He felt that maintaining some military production in Slovakia was necessary to avoid social upheaval.

The new doctrine builds on earlier efforts in the 1960s to create a nationally oriented Czechoslovak military doctrine, and it is based on two main concepts: (1) It is defensive in all aspects, and (2) it envisions no specific enemy. A Czechoslovak civilian participant commented that the process of devising a new doctrine was a new experience, since previously the Ministry of Defense simply put into practice the concepts outlined to them by the Soviets. Eliminating the previous anti-NATO orientation of the Czechoslovak armed force has required the Czechoslovak military to undertake a massive relocation of forces in line with the new doctrine. This includes remilitarizing Slovakia and reducing troops in the Czech lands, especially in Bohemia.

Czechoslovakia is not alone in adopting the concept of all-around defense as the main aspect of declaratory defense policy. The same concept had been adopted even earlier by Poland and Hungary. However, as a U.S. civilian participant noted, the idea is more sustainable in Czechoslovakia than in Poland because Czechoslovakia is smaller and in a more favorable geographical setting, due to its greater length and the Western protruding shape of its border with Germany and Austria.

Some U.S. participants viewed the Czechoslovak military doctrine as an evolutionary step and one that reflected only partial understanding of the changes that had taken place since 1989. The doctrine seemed a throwback to Czechoslovak deliberations in the mid-1960s, and it seemed more suited to a neutral country between two major alliances than to a Europe where the major enemy is uncertainty. The discussions regarding the doctrine provided another example of the difficulty Czechoslovak officials had in accepting the need for a total break with the past and in adjusting to a totally new security environment in the 1990s.

An important component of Czechoslovak plans for future military reform is Plan 2005, a blueprint for the military through 2005. Plan 2005 envisions a largely professional, much smaller, but more modern military. Professionalization has been a contentious issue in civil-military relations in Czechoslovakia, and the conference showed evidence of some residual differences of opinion on the topic among Czechoslovak participants. For example, a Czechoslovak military spokesman noted that implementing Plan 2005 depends on future developments in Europe. According to him, the pace of shifting to a professional military depends on favorable domestic and international conditions.

He also added that in the near future, a professional military would not be feasible for economic reasons—it simply would not meet current defense tasks at an affordable cost.

Another question that came up was the combat readiness of the Czechoslovak military. Many junior officers had not been satisfied with their conditions of life in the military, and they left en masse following the political changes, i.e., once they could leave the military without fearing sanctions. Similarly, far-reaching provisions of the law on military service (adopted in spring 1990) allowed conscripts to opt for alternative service while already in the military. As a Czechoslovak civilian participant acknowledged, the quality of training had suffered and there has been a serious shortage of personnel, both junior officers and conscripts. As a result, in October 1990, many understrength units were disbanded and joined with others to achieve full strength.

Czechoslovak participants had no illusions about the military potential of their country. A Czechoslovak military spokesman said bluntly that Czechoslovakia could not mount a long-term defense in the face of an invasion by a larger aggressor force. A Czechoslovak civilian added that the political realm offered much more hope in terms of security than the military, for the armed forces were constrained by their relatively limited material, operational, and economic potential. Again, this line of argument led to Czechoslovak advocacy for further institutionalizing the CSCE.

4. CONCLUSIONS

The central conclusion that can be drawn from the workshop is that the Czechoslovak military has evolved greatly toward a genuine state institution since the political changes in late 1989. However, Czechoslovak officials look to the United States (as well as other Western countries) for assistance in training personnel, both uniformed military as well as civilian security experts. Such help would ensure the continued successful transformation of the Czechoslovak military.

The institutions that formulate national security policy as well as the mechanisms for civilian oversight of the military are still being modified. In some areas the progress is greater than in others. For example, the Czechoslovak federal National Security Council (a decision-making body rather than an advisory body) is still very much in its infancy. Similarly, the division of powers between the Federal Assembly and the Office of the President regarding the control and oversight of the military still seems unclear. On the other hand, parliamentary control over the military is quite extensive, though Czechoslovak officials look to the United States Congress for more advice and assistance in further shaping their relationship with the military.

The problems of limited defense awareness and widespread anti-military perceptions among the population in Czechoslovakia must be surmounted in order to achieve a greater degree of security and normally functioning civil-military relations. In this context, Czechoslovak officials welcome any U.S. advice and documents on civil-military relations.

The workshop took place before the August 1991 coup attempt in Moscow that marked the end of Communist dictatorship in the former USSR. Czechoslovak apprehensions of Soviet designs on Eastern Europe have calmed since that time. However, the sense of unease regarding instability and potential spillover of ethnic strife from the Ukraine into Slovakia has probably increased. The disintegration of Yugoslavia during the summer of 1991 as well as the potential for the spread of the conflict (through the involvement of Hungary, for example) have emerged as real threats to stability in the region. These developments are bound to motivate Czechoslovak officials to continue to further institutionalize CSCE and to attain security guarantees through membership in Western security organizations. The United

States can play a moderating force by assuaging some of the Czechoslovak fears through greater engagement with Czechoslovakia in the security realm. The changed international situation as a result of the Soviet collapse favors such an evolution.

Appendix A
LIST OF PARTICIPANTS

U.S. Participants

John A. Baker, Atlantic Council of the United States

Walter Christman, U.S. Department of Defense

George L. Donohue, RAND

Major General Waldo D. Freeman, Jr., U.S. Army

A. Ross Johnson, Radio Free Europe/Radio Liberty Research Institute

Vladimir V. Kusin, Radio Free Europe/Radio Liberty
Research Institute

F. Stephen Larrabee, RAND

Brigadier General B. L. Mitchell, U.S. Air Force

Colonel Daniel Painter, U.S. Embassy, Prague

Major Donald Palendech, U.S. Air Force

Major General Cloyd Pfister, U.S. Army

Steven W. Popper, RAND

General Robert H. Reed, U.S. Air Force (Ret.),
National Training Systems Association

Walter B. Slocombe, Caplin & Drysdale Chartered

James B. Steinberg, RAND

Thomas S. Szayna, RAND

William Taylor, United States Mission to NATO

James A. Thomson, RAND

CSFR Participants

Lieutenant General Imrich Andrejcak, Deputy Minister of National Defense

Miloslav Blahout, Member of Federal Assembly

Svatopluk Buchlovsky, Federal Ministry of Foreign Affairs

Major General Stanislav Chromec, CSFR Army

Vladimir Cebis, Institute of International Relations

Stanislava Hubnerova, Charles University

Jaroslav Janda, Deputy Vice-Minister of National Defense

Colonel Ladislav Klima, Ministry of National Defense

Josef Knobloch, Institute of International Relations

Colonel Imrich Kucera, Bratislava Military College

Vladimir Leska, Institute of International Relations

Lt. Col. Eduard Miklas, Bratislava Military College

Zdenek Nejedly, Federal Ministry of Foreign Affairs

Alexandr Ort, Charles University

Miroslav Purkrabek, Adviser to the Minister of National Defense

Laszlo Rajczy, Member of Federal Assembly

Jan Solc, Member of Federal Assembly

Milan Stembera, Institute of International Relations

Jiri Stepanovsky, Institute of International Relations

Jiri Valenta, Institute of International Relations

Alexandr Vondra, Adviser to the President of CSFR

Appendix B
AGENDA

Sunday, May 5, 1991

    19:00   Dinner hosted by the CSFR Foreign Ministry at the Cerninsky Palace

Monday, May 6, 1991

    9:00–9:30   Conference Opening/Welcoming Remarks

    9:30–12:30   Session 1: Civil-Military Relations in the CSFR and United States—Establishing Civilian Control of the Military

                        The Evolution of the CSFR National Security-Making Process Since November 1989

                        U.S. Perspectives on Civil-Military Relations: The Role of the Secretary of Defense and the Military

    12:30–14:30   Lunch

    14:30–17:00   Session 2: Civil-Military Relations— Defining National Goals and Policies

                        Civil-Military Relations: the Interagency Process

                        The Role of Parliament/Congress

    17:30–19:00   U.S. Embassy reception, hosted by U.S. Ambassador

    20:00   Dinner hosted by RAND at Hotel Budovatel

Tuesday, May 7, 1991

    9:30–12:00   Session 3: CSFR and U.S. Perspectives on Security in Central Europe

                        CSFR Approach to Security in Europe

                        Evolving NATO Doctrine for Europe

12:00–12:30	Summary and Concluding Remarks
12:30	Lunch
14:30	End of conference